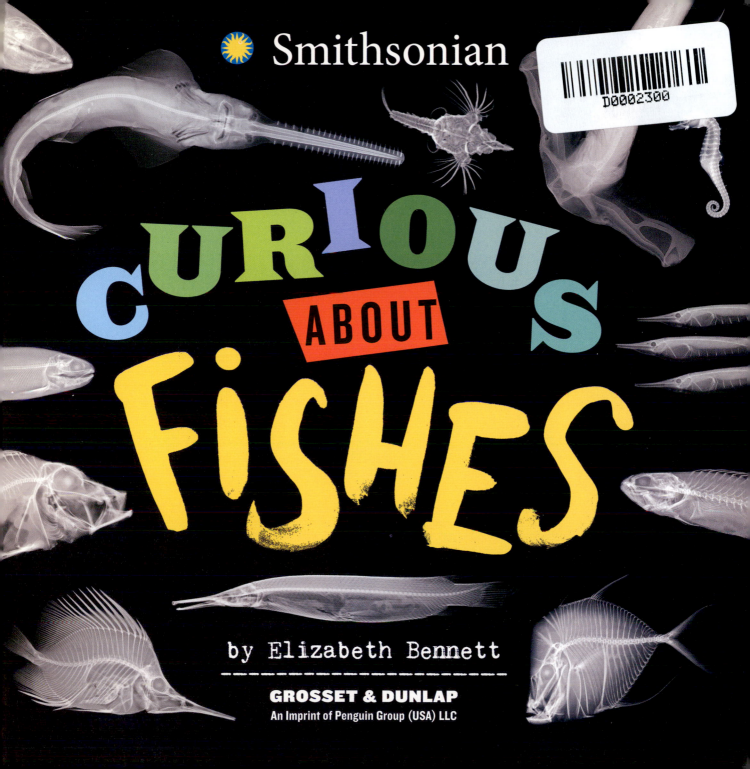

☀ **Smithsonian**

CURIOUS
ABOUT
FISHES

by Elizabeth Bennett

GROSSET & DUNLAP
An Imprint of Penguin Group (USA) LLC

GROSSET & DUNLAP

Published by the Penguin Group
Penguin Group (USA) LLC, 375 Hudson Street, New York, New York 10014, USA

USA | Canada | UK | Ireland | Australia | New Zealand | India | South Africa | China

penguin.com
A Penguin Random House Company

 Smithsonian

This trademark is owned by the Smithsonian Institution and
is registered in the U.S. Patent and Trademark Office.

Smithsonian Enterprises:
Christopher Liedel, President
Carol LeBlanc, Senior Vice President, Education and Consumer Products
Brigid Ferraro, Vice President, Education and Consumer Products
Ellen Nanney, Licensing Manager
Kealy Gordon, Product Development Manager

Smithsonian Institution, National Museum of Natural History:
Sandra J. Raredon, Museum Specialist
Carole Baldwin, Curator of Fishes
Lynne R. Parenti, PhD, Curator of Fishes and Research Scientist

PHOTO CREDITS: All X-rays (cover, interiors) and specimens (pages 30–31): Sandra J. Raredon,
Museum Specialist, National Museum of Natural History, © 2015 Smithsonian Institution. All other photographs
from Thinkstock/© individual photographers. Page 3: top left: BLUEXHAND, center left: Dovapi, top right: Moodboard,
center right: Becca Vogt; page 4: Marilyn Haddrill; page 6: voltanl; page 8: left & right: Eric Isselée, center: GlobalP;
page 9: Dave Bluck; page 10: IPG Gutenberg UK, Ltd; page 12: Lilith Lita; page 14: Tane-mahuta; page 16: Ian Scott;
page 17: Moodboard; page 18: Josh Bishop; page 19: Nick Po; page 20–21: Shaun Wilkinson; page 22: 578foot;
page 23: FtLaudGirl; page 24: Comstock Images; page 25: Roger de Marfà; page 26: Iliuta Goean; page 28: singularone.

Library of Congress Cataloging-in-Publication Data is available.

ISBN 978-0-448-48462-4   10 9 8 7 6 5 4 3 2 1

Tiny seahorses.
Toothy sharks.
Wiggly eels and
"winged" rays.

They're all

FiSHES!

More than thirty thousand different kinds
of fishes swim around in underwater worlds.
So what makes a fish a fish? Some of the
answers are in the X-rays! An X-ray is a special
photograph that shows the inside of something.

    Let's look inside some fishes to see how
they work.

Fishes are **vertebrates**, which are animals with backbones. A backbone helps support an animal's body and gives it length. Backbones are made up of many separate pieces called **vertebrae** (say: **VER**-teh-bray).

This **striped bass** has a long backbone. At one end is the skull, where you can see the jawbones and the eye **socket**. At the other end, you can see the smaller vertebrae that form the tail.

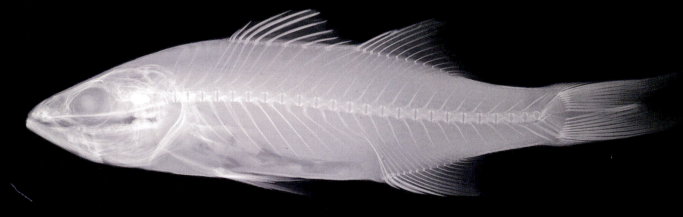

FISH FACT The striped bass gets its name from the dark stripes on its body. This fish lives in the ocean but releases its eggs in freshwater rivers.

If a backbone gives a fish length, ribs help give it shape—and shape can give it a name!

Ribs are connected to the vertebrae at the head end of the backbone. The **hatchetfish** gets its name from its really long ribs. They form the "blade" of the hatchet. The backbone at the tail end of this fish forms the "handle."

Big, small—all fishes swim!
Many fishes move through water
by **flexing** their bodies, fluttering their
fins, and swishing their tails. Thin bones
called rays form the skeleton of a fish's
fins. Fins along the top and bottom of
a fish help it stay balanced in the water
as it swims. Pairs of side fins help it start,
stop, and steer. Many fishes use their tail fins
to push themselves forward while using their
muscles to move their bodies from side to side.

tropical gar

The top or **dorsal** fin on this **crisscross prickleback** is very long. Its spiny rays are sharp and prickly, which is how this fish got its name.

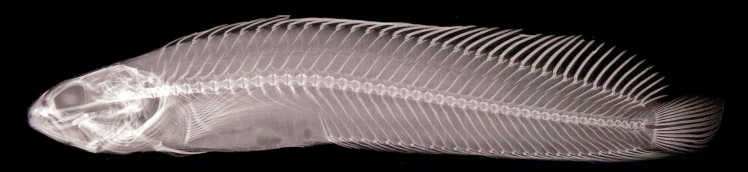

The **tropical gar** is another fish with a long dorsal fin. It also has a very strong tail, or **caudal** fin.

A **seahorse** uses its fins and tail to swim in an upright position. It moves its horselike head back and forth to steer. But this is not a very fast way to get around!

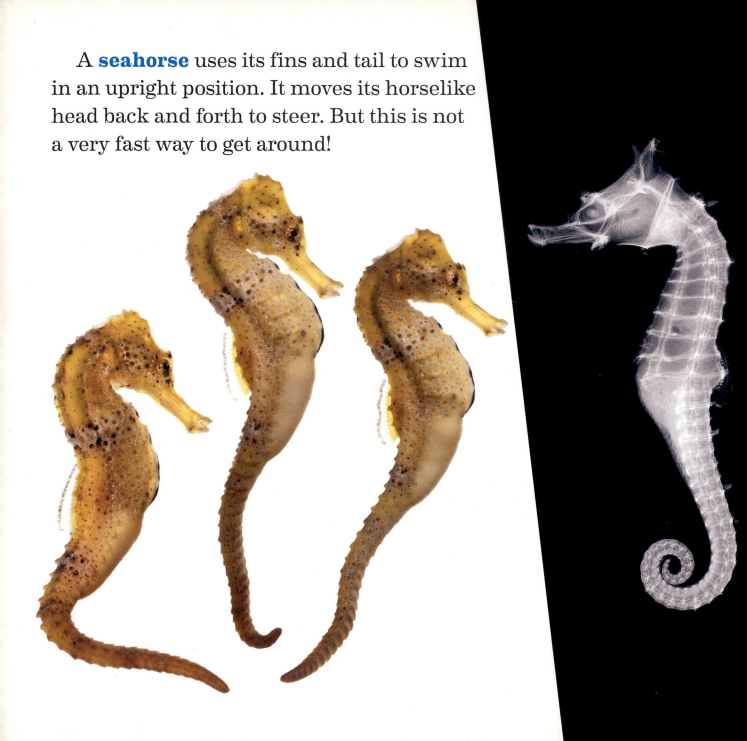

Fishes that swim slowly, like seahorses, use **camouflage** to protect themselves from **predators**. Some seahorses can change color to blend in—and escape being fish food.

A seahorse holds on to seaweed tightly with its tail. As it sways in the ocean **currents**, it looks just like seaweed. Hungry fishes swim right on by!

snappers, with gills

Like other animals, fishes need oxygen. So how do they get that underwater?

Gills.

As a fish swims, it takes in water through its mouth. That water is filtered through its gills, **organs** with slits on either side of the fish. As the water flows over the gills, the fish's blood absorbs oxygen from the water. A fish's skeleton includes a hinged, bony plate that opens and closes. This plate protects the gills. You can see it in this **red dory** under the eye socket.

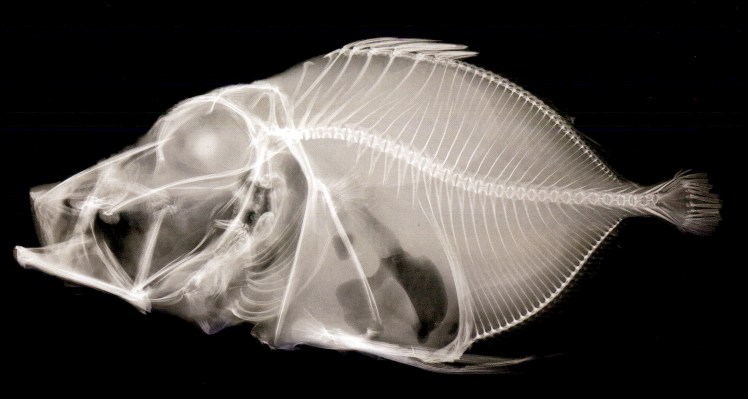

Many fishes have bony skeletons. Others, including rays, skates, and sharks, have skeletons made of **cartilage**. Cartilage is a tough, rubbery, flexible tissue. Pinch your nose or ears, and you'll feel cartilage!

blue-spotted stingray

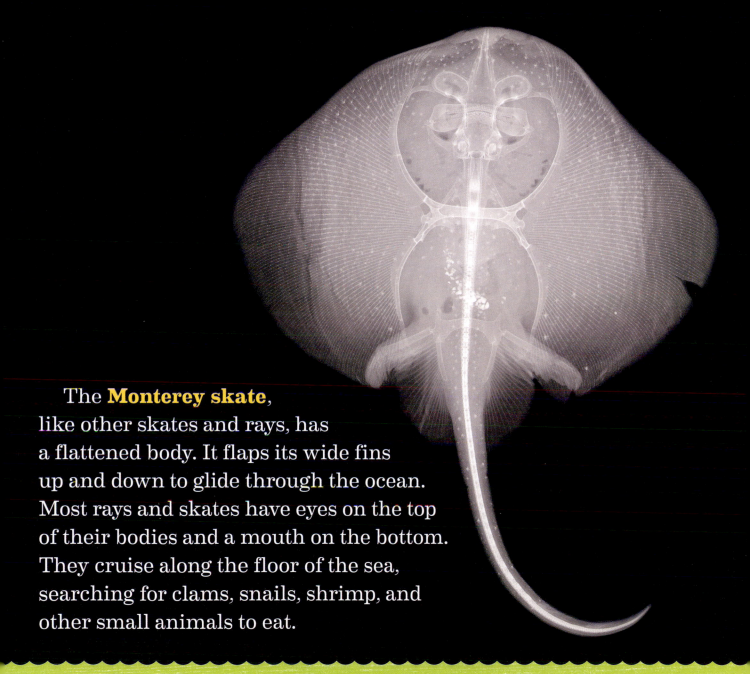

The **Monterey skate**,
like other skates and rays, has
a flattened body. It flaps its wide fins
up and down to glide through the ocean.
Most rays and skates have eyes on the top
of their bodies and a mouth on the bottom.
They cruise along the floor of the sea,
searching for clams, snails, shrimp, and
other small animals to eat.

FISH FACT Fossils of skates and rays prove that these animals have been around since prehistoric times!

Fishes need to look for food—and watch out so they don't *become* food! Many of them, like this **lookdown fish**, have eyes on each side so they can see in two directions at once. As you can see, with its low mouth and high eyes, this fish appears to "look down." Fishes' eyes are specially designed to help them see underwater, where light can vary.

Some fishes, like flounders and batfishes, are flat. These fishes lie on the sandy bottom of the ocean, often buried and hidden. Flounders lie on one side of their bodies. Their eyes are on the other side. Batfishes lie on their bellies. Their eyes are on top. Peering up with both eyes helps them spot a meal swimming overhead!

The **pancake batfish** uses its fins to crawl along the ocean floor searching for food. This tiny fish, small enough to fit in a person's hand, got its name from its round shape—like a pancake.

 Flounders are born with an eye on each side. One eye gradually moves to the other side as the young fish matures.

This shark has one eye—*and* one nostril—
on each side of its "hammer"!

hammerhead shark

Winghead sharks are members of the hammerhead shark family. It is believed that the shape of their heads and the positions of their eyes and nostrils give these fishes very strong senses of sight and smell. This helps these sharks track fast-moving **prey**. And even better—their hammer-shaped heads help them turn very quickly so they can catch smaller fishes!

FISH FACT When a shark loses a tooth in a front row, a tooth from the second row moves forward to replace it.

rainbow trout

When it comes to chasing food, shape matters!
Fishes that swim fast, like this **rainbow trout**,
tend to have long, **tapered** bodies.

Their strong tails and torpedo-like
shape mean they can race through
currents in search of food.

FISH FACT The rainbow trout is named for its blue-green or yellow-green coloring and pink side streaks.

Here's another fish named for something you might find in a toolbox. And this one cuts up its food!

The **snout** of a **smalltooth sawfish** has a long, flat blade with about twenty teeth on each side.

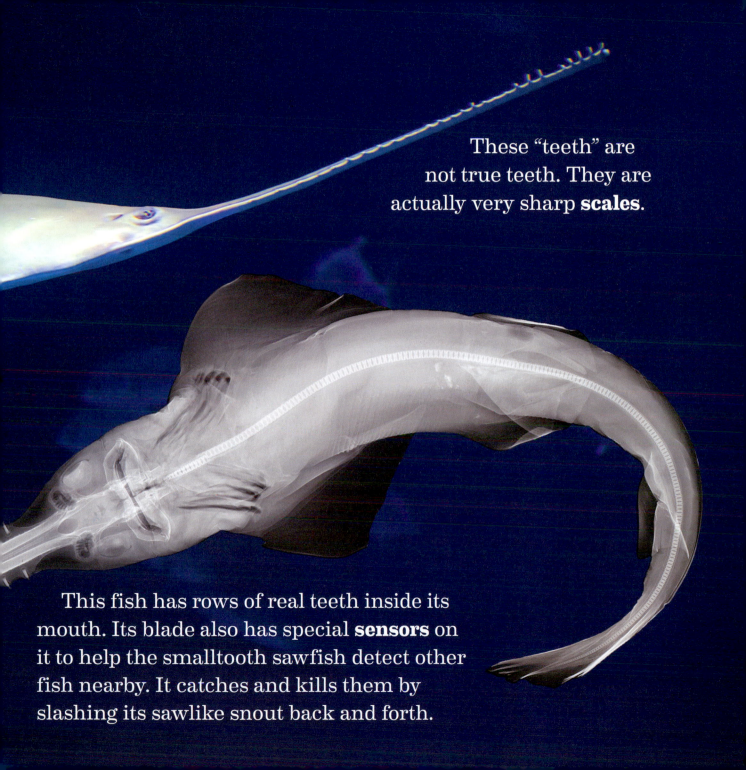

These "teeth" are not true teeth. They are actually very sharp **scales**.

This fish has rows of real teeth inside its mouth. Its blade also has special **sensors** on it to help the smalltooth sawfish detect other fish nearby. It catches and kills them by slashing its sawlike snout back and forth.

Some fishes are good hunters, thanks to their shapes.
Other fishes are good fighters.

long-spined porcupine fish

The **long-spined porcupine fish** has flat, needlelike spines all over its body. When it feels threatened by a predator, it swallows water or gulps air to blow up like a big fat balloon. And if size isn't enough to scare off the other fishes, the porcupine fish's sharp spines are quite dangerous when it's puffed up.

Once the threat passes, the porcupine fish shrinks back to its normal size. Its large eyes help it look out for the next risky situation.

Eels are another kind of fish with bodies built for protection. Long and snakelike, they can easily slither into cracks between rocks and in coral reefs. These hiding spots protect eels from predators and let them sneak up on prey.

moray eel

Moray eels make their homes in coral reefs and shallow waters near the coast in warm oceans. They can grow to about thirteen feet long. Like other fishes, moray eels breathe through gills and use pairs of fins to swim. But they don't have scales like other fishes. Their bodies are protected by a thick layer of mucus.

FISH FACT There are as many as two hundred different types of moray eels, and they all have one thing in common: very sharp teeth!

Fishes smell!
Really, they do. Fishes don't have noses, but they do have nostrils, located on their snouts. They use their sense of smell to help find food, flee enemies, or find a mate.

longnose butterflyfish

This bright yellow **longnose butterflyfish** has a very long snout and mouth. It sucks up food that it finds in the tropical seaweed reefs where it makes its home. While it has a good sense of smell like other fishes, the butterflyfish still depends more on sight than smell. This is because scents in the water can float away with the current.

FISH FACT Some sharks can smell a single drop of blood in the water from one quarter-mile away!

Why do some fishes go to school? For protection!

A large group of fish is called a school. A little fish swimming in a big school has a much better chance of surviving than if it were swimming alone.

rigid shrimpfish

Schools of fish, like these **rigid shrimpfish**, swim together in a tight pattern and often change direction. This confuses a hungry predator. It doesn't know where to bite first!

Fishes also search for food in schools. When a few fish in a school start eating, the others do, too.

The X-rays and other photos in this book show the important things that make a fish a fish. But they also show interesting differences among fishes.

Scientists use a **classification** system to keep track of this kind of information. Living things with similar features are grouped together. (Fishes are part of the animal kingdom.) Every living thing is given a scientific name.

Below are the actual fish **specimens** from which the X-rays in this book were made. Their scientific names are in blue.

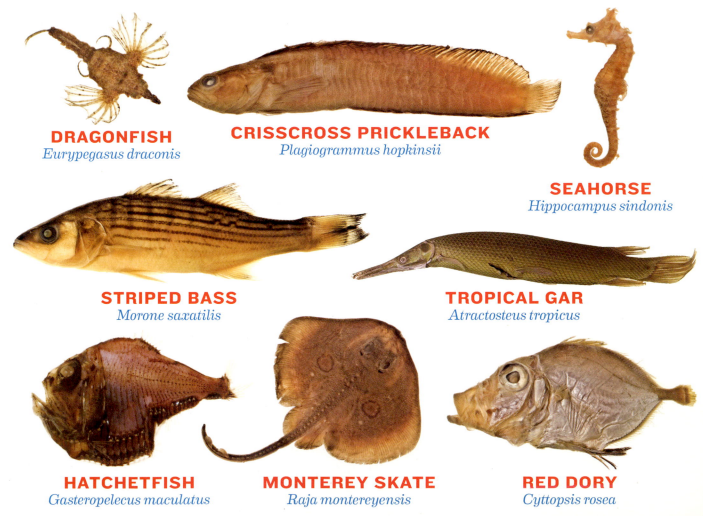

DRAGONFISH
Eurypegasus draconis

CRISSCROSS PRICKLEBACK
Plagiogrammus hopkinsii

SEAHORSE
Hippocampus sindonis

STRIPED BASS
Morone saxatilis

TROPICAL GAR
Atractosteus tropicus

HATCHETFISH
Gasteropelecus maculatus

MONTEREY SKATE
Raja montereyensis

RED DORY
Cyttopsis rosea

LOOKDOWN FISH
Selene vomer

WINGHEAD SHARK
Eusphyra blochii

SMALLTOOTH SAWFISH
Pristis pectinata

PANCAKE BATFISH
Halieutichthys aculeatus

LONG-SPINED PORCUPINE FISH
Diodon holocanthus

RAINBOW TROUT
Oncorhynchus mykiss

VIPER MORAY EEL
Enchelynassa canina

RIGID SHRIMPFISH
Centriscus scutatus

LONGNOSE BUTTERFLYFISH
Forcipiger longirostris

GLOSSARY

camouflage: coloring or covering that makes animals or objects look like their surroundings

cartilage: a strong elastic tissue found in humans and animals

caudal: on or near the tail

classification: putting things into groups according to their characteristics

current: the movement of water in an ocean, river, or large lake

dorsal: on the back

flex: to bend or stretch something

gill: the organ on a fish's side through which it breathes

organ: a part of the body that does a particular job

predator: an animal that lives by hunting other animals for food

prey: an animal that is hunted by other animals for food

scale: one of the small pieces of hard skin that covers the body of a fish or reptile

sensor: something that can detect changes in heat, sound, or pressure

snout: the long front part of an animal's head that includes the nose, mouth, and jaws

socket: a hole or hollow place where something fits inside

specimen: an example of a plant or animal

tapered: becomes narrow at one end

vertebrae: the small bones that make up the backbone

vertebrate: an animal with a backbone

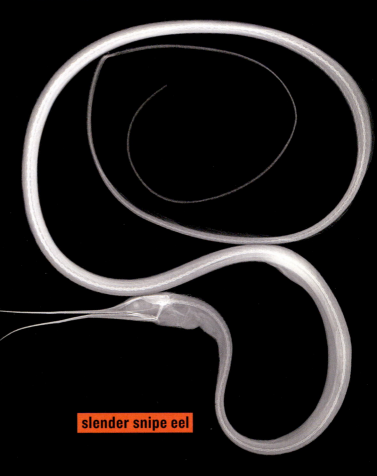

slender snipe eel